PICTURE THE WORLD
WORKING TRUCKS

AWARD PUBLICATIONS LIMITED

Fighting the fire

Emergency! There's a fire at No 10 Bay Road. The bell rings in the fire station. The fire-fighters start up the fire engine, drive out of the station and race to the scene of the fire. Then out come the hoses and jets of water are directed on to the blaze. From inside the building there are cries for help. A fireman climbs to the rescue wearing air tanks so that he can breathe in fresh air.

Moving heavy loads

Very careful planning is needed before a heavy load can be taken by road from one place to another. It is necessary to check that the roads on the planned route are wide enough and straight enough for the load to pass through. The police must be warned of possible delays to other road-users as the load moves by. If the load is especially wide, heavy, or slow-moving, motor-cycle police will probably travel with it on its journey.

The concrete mixer

Builders use concrete, which is made of cement, sand, small stones and water. The concrete mixer is loaded with these at a special place called a batching plant. The revolving drum mixes the cement as the lorry drives along so that the concrete is ready when it arrives at the building site. The concrete is unloaded down a chute where the builders need it.

The tanker

Some lorries are specially made to carry liquids of one kind or another. These lorries are called tankers. A tanker might carry oil, petrol or chemicals. If the cargo is dangerous, there will be notices on the sides and back warning people to stay clear. The tank of a milk tanker is lined with glass.

After a breakdown

Sometimes a vehicle breaks down and is unable to go any further under its own power. Then the breakdown truck, or tow truck is sent for. The breakdown truck has a small crane at the back and this lifts the front of the broken-down vehicle off the ground. The truck can then tow it on its rear wheels to a garage where the vehicle can be repaired. Some breakdown trucks can also carry the vehicle's passengers as well.

The road-train

Australia is a vast country and there are large parts of it where towns are long distances away from each other. The road-train is used to deliver goods to distant places like this. A road-train is made up of a very strong driving unit pulling three or even four large trailers, each with many wheels to carry the weight. Thundering along the long, straight roads of the Australian outback, these road-trains are a familiar sight.

Clearing the snow

In those parts of the world that have heavy snowfalls, snowploughs are used to keep the roads passable. A snowplough is a heavy-duty lorry with a plough blade on the front. As the lorry drives along the snow-covered road, the plough blade cuts into the snow and pushes it away on each side. The snowplough sprays a layer of road salt behind it which stops the road from becoming icy.

Skip truck

ISBN 0 - 86163 - 969 - 3

Copyright © 1999 Award Publications Limited

First published 1999
Second impression 2002
Third impression 2006

Published by Award Publications Limited,
The Old Riding School, The Welbeck Estate,
Worksop, Nottinghamshire S80 3LR

Printed in Singapore